Discover
Rodents

by Victoria Marcos

© 2018 by Victoria Macos
ISBN: 978-1-53240-541-9
eISBN: 978-1-53240-542-6
Images licensed from AdobeStock.com
All rights reserved.
No portion of this book may be reproduced without express permission of the publisher.
First Edition
Published in the United States by
Xist Publishing
www.xistpublishing.com
PO Box 61593 Irvine, CA 92602

Rodents are small to medium size mammals that gnaw on things. Their teeth always keep growing.

Beavers live in North America, Europe, and Asia. They are known for building dams. Beavers knock down trees and use the wood as building material and for food. They also use dams to protect themselves from predators.

Capybaras are the largest rodents in the world. They live in savannas and forests near water in South America. Capybaras are herbivores that eat mostly grasses and aquatic plants.

5

Chinchillas live in burrows in the Andes Mountains in South America.

In the wild, chinchillas eat plants, seeds, fruit, and small insects.

They are excellent jumpers. They can jump up to six feet.

Chipmunks eat mostly nuts, seeds, fruit, and flower buds. Eastern chipmunks hibernate in the winter. Since western chipmunks don't hibernate, they store food in their burrows which they eat in the cold winter months.

Ferrets spend 14-18 hours a day sleeping. When they're awake they're very social and live in groups called "businesses." Ferrets are very playful. They'll invite you to play by hopping around sideways and making a sound that sounds like a honk.

Groundhogs live in the North American lowlands. They mostly eat grasses, berries, and sometimes small insects and animals. Groundhogs are excellent swimmers and can climb trees to escape predators.

Guinea pigs are not from Guinea nor are they pigs. Like chinchillas, guinea pigs are also from the Andes Mountains. They eat grasses and other vegetation. They don't make their own nests. Instead, they live in the burrows of other animals.

Wild hamsters live underground and stay there during the day to avoid predators. They mostly eat seeds, vegetation, fruit, and sometimes small insects. They carry food in their cheek pouches back to their burrows.

Hutia live in the Caribbean Islands. Most species are herbivores and eat roots, leaves, stems, and bark. Unlike most other animals, hutias get all their water from food. They make their nests in trees, caves, or rock crevices.

19

Jerboas are hopping desert rodents found in Northern Africa and Asia.

Jerboas are nocturnal. During the day, they sleep in burrows under the hot desert sand. At night when it's cool they leave their burrows to eat. They mostly eat plants, but some species will also eat insects.

When chased by a predator, jerboas can run as fast as 15 mph.

Jirds make their home in semi-desert areas in dry rocky hillsides in Northern Africa and the Middle East. They find shelter in burrows or under rocks. They eat grains and dry plants and sometimes small insects.

Lemmings live in or near the Arctic. They burrow in the snow to find food and for protection from predators. They eat grasses, leaves, roots, and flower bulbs which they store in their burrows. Lemmings are solitary animals which means they live alone.

25

Meerkats live in only a few African deserts. They mostly eat insects, but will also eat small animals and mushrooms. They stand on their hind legs to keep a look out for predators. When they see one, they bark. The other meerkats run underground and hide.

Mice exist in almost every part of the world. They are herbivores eating mostly grains and fruit. Mice that live in the city will eat almost any kind of food. In the wild they build complex burrows with many tunnels.

Porcupines live in a few parts of the world. They have sharp quills that help defend them against predators. They eat leaves and twigs and in the winter they eat bark.

Squirrels live in many places. Although squirrels usually eat nuts, seeds, and plants, they sometimes eat insects, eggs, and young snakes.

www.ingramcontent.com/pod-product-compliance
Lightning Source LLC
LaVergne TN
LVHW010317070426
835507LV00026B/3438